100 Things

Every Online Student Ought to Know

A self-orientation guide with definitions, customs, procedures, and advice to assist students in adjusting to taking online courses.

by Frank L. Christ and Loyd R. Ganey Jr., Ph.D.

Cambridge Stratford Study Skills Institute - Williamsville, NY

100 Things Every Online Student Ought to Know

by Frank L. Christ and Loyd R. Ganey Jr., Ph.D.

Copyright © 2003
The Cambridge Stratford Study Skills Institute
A division of Cambridge Stratford, Ltd.
8560 Main Street, Williamsville, New York 14221

The
Cambridge-Stratford
Study Skills
Institute

Library of Congress Number: 2003108673
ISBN: 0-935637-30-3   Printed in the USA
Printing is the lowest number: 10 9 8 7 6 5 4 3 2 1

Acknowledgements

Dr. Ganey and Frank Christ would like to thank the following colleagues and friends.

For Dr. Ganey, thanks to Dr. Bill Percy (Capella University), Dr. Pam Patrick (Capella University), and Bill Akins (Online Campus Director, Cochise College) for their support and inspiration in distance education. Many thanks go to Leslie Clark, Meredith Anderson and Gerlinde Ganey for excellent proofreading.

For Frank Christ, thanks to Dr. Gwyn Enright for her comments on the manuscript and to Alice Christ for her perceptive proofing.

For both Dr. Ganey and Frank Christ the ultimate thank you goes out to hundreds of online students who have been a great source of learning and have offered many generous comments and suggestions to help all online learners thrive and succeed.

Who Are The Authors?

Dr. Loyd Ray Ganey Jr. is Faculty/Mentor for Western Governors University, Professor and Campus Chair for Behavioral Sciences at Western International University, and also serves as a BlackBoard Systems Administrator and Online Educator for Cochise College. He has been very active in distance education for the past seven years as a student, course developer, and instructor; and earned a professional certificate in instructional design for online learning from Capella University. Dr. Ganey consults with several colleges on distance education and continues to make presentations at the local, state and national levels on distance education. Dr. Ganey completed a Ph.D. in Human Services from Capella University, an M.S. in Professional Counseling from Georgia State University, an M.DIV. from Abilene Christian University, and a dual B.A. in Humanities Interdisciplinary Studies and Religious Studies from the University of West Florida. Dr. Ganey is a retired U.S. Army Chaplain and is also a published author. His recent publications include several ancillaries for Wadsworth/Thomson Learning in the Behavioral Sciences and *Becoming a Successful Distance Learner: Eight Readiness Factors* with H&H Publishing. Dr. Ganey enjoys setting up online learners for success.

Frank Christ has been associated with higher education for the past 50 years as an instructor and administrator at Loyola College (Baltimore), St. Vincent College (Latrobe, PA), Loyola Marymount University (Los Angeles), and CSU Long Beach (California). Currently, he is a Visiting Scholar (University of Arizona), and an Adjunct Professor at Grambling State University, Louisiana where he teaches online graduate courses in learning assistance. He has also been a consultant in learning skills and learning center design for colleges and universities, for business and industry, and for secondary schools and districts. Frank has been involved in student learning support for the past 25 years as a learning assistance center administrator, learning skills facilitator, staff trainer, learning center consultant, online learning skills facilitator, graduate course instructor, author, editor, conference keynoter and presenter. His teaching, professional presentations and publications are currently focused on the development of academic support for online students. Frank has received numerous educational awards including a Lifetime Achievement Award (1993) from Association of California Community Colleges for Tutoring and Learning Assistance and the Jade Award (2002) from College Reading and Learning Association for 35 years of service. In 1999, Frank was inducted as an American Council of Developmental Education Associations Founding Fellow in Learning Assistance.

Introduction

Attention! Please read this before going forward.

One of the most critical skills for the online student is reading. Why? Because the independent nature of online learning requires a student to read, comprehend, and follow directions explicitly. There will be more within this book on this skill and many others that will empower you, the online student, and set you up for success in the online learning environment. Stay tuned and read on!

This book provides practical information, which will not only offer empowering tidbits to enhance your online learning experience, but will also greatly assure your success in the online environment. Much of the information you will capture from this book comes from the authors' experience as online students, online course developers/designers, and online course educators. We have also gathered feedback from hundreds of online students across the nation and the world.

Online learning is growing at an exponential rate. Online learning is becoming increasingly popular as economic and educational forces change and encourage new technologies to facilitate newer ways of learning. The number and types of individuals pursuing learning outside traditional classrooms are experiencing phenomenal growth. The overwhelming majority of online students are working adults who are juggling work, family, and academic/professional goals. Online students pursue online learning due to the convenience and flexibility it provides. Online learning can eliminate travel and scheduling constraints, and most importantly it can increase access to higher education. The appeal of lifelong learning has stimulated many adults to return to college and pursue courses, degrees, and certificate programs. As the costs of computers and other electronic devices decrease, more students will be able to take advantage of these courses and programs.

Online learning is becoming increasingly global, creating a myriad of new partnerships as traditional educational institutions join with businesses, foreign governments, and international organizations to offer and use online learning. The Internet is transforming the world into a borderless educational arena where students can willfully pursue specific courses, complete degrees, and specialized and professional certificates.

Internet connectivity of colleges and universities has been one of the most dramatic changes in educational history. Online learning is emerging as an increasingly important component of higher education and is becoming part and parcel of academic programs throughout the United States. Today thousands of colleges and universities provide millions of students with online programs. Currently, online learning programs in 2 and 4-year academic institutions are growing at an annual rate of 15%. Enrollments in Online learning programs are over 2 million students annually. The Integrated Postsecondary Education Data System (IPEDS) College Opportunities Online http://nces.ed.gov/ipeds/cool/Search.asp is a direct search link to over 9,000 institutions of higher education in the United States, ranging from a large university to a small liberal arts college, a specialized college, a community college, a career or technical college or a trade school. Telecampus http://courses.telecampus.edu/subjects/index.cfm is a directory of over 60,000 online courses, programs and tutorials.

Reading this book will give you the awareness of skills and knowledge hundreds of online students before you have discovered as being essential to their survival and success. Some of the *100 Things Every Online Student Ought to Know* will require further inquiry and investigation. You are encouraged to accent your areas of strength and conduct further research in those areas requiring more skill development and/or knowledge. We will include some websites to assist you in this endeavor.

We have categorized the items, but the layout is not in sequential importance. Some of the topical areas may overlap and you can use the index to locate specific information. For your convenience at the end of some of the 100 Things, you may find a box enclosing a reference to a website or to a specific web page. Please note that as of the publication of this book, all of the URLs (web addresses) referenced were accessible. However, it does happen that at some time in the future, one or more of these URLS (web addresses) may be discontinued or changed so that when you try to access them you see a message on the screen indicating that they are not accessible.

We welcome your reactions and comments. An Editorial Contribution form is attached at the end. Please share your comments so other online students in the future can learn from your online experiences.

Remember the intent of the book is to empower you, the online student, to be successful as you pursue online courses. So, roll up your sleeves and delve into the practical *100 Things Every Online Student Ought to Know*.

Table of Contents

Online Facts

Online Students Ought to Know:

1.   that **the number of online degree programs and online courses is growing at a phenomenal rate**. According to the National Center for Educational Statistics, an arm of the U.S. Department of Education, the number of distance education programs at U.S. colleges and universities grew by 72 percent between 1995 and 1998 or from 860 to nearly 1200 programs. Farhad Saba, professor of educational technology at San Diego State University and CEO of Distance-Educator.com, says that businesses will invest over $30 billion into distance educa-

tion in 2002. What does this mean to you, the online student? Well, the number and variety of online courses and degree programs are growing at an exponential rate. This means you can willfully shop for those courses or degree programs that fit your academic, career, or life goals, and do so from your home.

National Center for Educational Statistics http://www.nces.ed.gov/
Distance-Educator.Com http://www.distance-educator.com/

Online Students Ought to Know:

2.   that it is very **important to ensure your online program or online course is from a regionally accredited academic institution**. This is most crucial because we are talking about your time and your money! Also, of extreme importance is that you want a credible course, certificate, and/or degree. Watch out for diploma mills! It is imperative that you do your homework and verify that your course, certificate, or degree program is endorsed by one of the major accrediting associations. You can ask your college by whom it is accredited or investigate via the Internet. A great source of accredited academic institutions is the book *2002-2003 Accredited Institutions of Postsecondary Education* edited by Kenneth A. Von Alt and pub-

lished by the American Council on Education. This book is a comprehensive guide to institutions of higher learning that are accredited by national and regional accrediting agencies and includes more than 6,000 public, private, two-year, four-year, and vocational institutions of higher education throughout the United States.

Council for Higher Education Accreditation http://www.chea.org/
Regional Accrediting Organizations
http://www.chea.org/Directories/regional.cfm
Virtual University Gazette's FAQs on Distance Learning, Accreditation, and College Degrees
http://www.geteducated.com/articles/dlfaq.htm

Online Students Ought to Know:

3. that it **is possible to start and complete a degree, undergraduate and graduate, totally online**. Amazing, and very true! Many colleges are creating complete degree programs online where a student doesn't even have to set foot on a campus. The break from face to face (F2F) or traditional academic programs is creating an opportunity for a large population of learners who are working and juggling many other life demands. These online degree programs offer many possibilities for a broad range of learners who are seeking a degree for academic, career, or life goals. The fantastic thing about such

degree programs is that the convenience and flexibility are there to fit your busy schedule and lifestyle. There are many places to go in search of such online degree programs. Here are some:

Degree.Net http://www.degree.net/
Directory of Internet Universities
http://www.geteducated.com/dlsites.htm
Distance Learning: Online Degrees
http://distancelearn.about.com/mbody.htm?once=true&eLearners.Com http://www.elearners.com/
Yahoo! Directory>Distance Learning>Colleges and Universities
http://dir.yahoo.com/EducationDistance_LearningColleges_and_Universities/

Online Students Ought to Know:

4.   that **many colleges and universities have a special web site or at least some web pages focusing on online course information and support**. When shopping for your online courses or online degree programs, you may want to create a folder within your Favorites or Bookmarks to save those url's (website addresses). Most major colleges today have a website or Internet presence. Locate the homepage of the college in which you are interested and search its site to see if it has an Online Campus, Online Learning or Distance Education Program. Look through the site to see specifically what courses are

offered and what online student support and services are offered. Here are some examples:

Capella University
http://www.capella.edu/schools_home_page/final.asp
Cochise College http://xwing.cochise.edu/online-campus/
Kaplan College http://www.kaplancollege.com
Western Governors University http://www.wgu.edu
Western International University http://www.wintu.edu

Online Students Ought to Know:

5.   that **an online course is accessible anywhere, any-time**. Cool! And so true! Your online course can be accessed from computer labs and to most public libraries, as well as Internet Cafes, Kinkos, Starbucks, etc. Access is available any-where where there is an Internet connection. The excuse that your computer is down, frozen, sick does not apply here. As a proactive online student you can access your course from any computer with a modem (phone line). Probably one of the first things you want to do to make sure you are not bound to any

single computer is create a document file on your course. Name it, label it, and save it to a diskette. Example: SOC101Notes. The document can be a place to store vital information like—course url (web address), username, and password. This way you take your diskette and access your course anywhere, anytime, whether you are across town or in Timbuktu, Mali (Africa). You will be able to access your online courses from all over the USA, Europe (even a pub in Scotland), to the far corners of the globe.

Online Students Ought to Know:

6.   that **an online course is different from a traditional face to face (F2F) course**. While both modes of delivery are about learning, they are quite different. The majority of online students will tell you that they learn more in the online environment, and that the demands of an online course are by far more demanding than F2F courses. The content of online courses is just like F2F courses—weekly assignments, papers due at set dates, quizzes and exams, and interactivity/participation. Perhaps the primary difference is that the overriding responsibility of learning lies with you—the online student. Being a successful online student takes self-discipline and self-enforced time management.

Online Students Ought to Know:

7.   that **online courses are convenient and flexible**. The reason why distance education is growing at such a phenomenal rate lies right here—convenience and flexibility! Okay . . . raise your hand if you have a day job! Or juggling who knows how many things in your life! Students come into distance education because it fits their life demands and goals. Many, like you, live in geographical areas where it is impossible to continue education in a F2F mode because there are no local colleges in the area, or the local colleges do not offer the academic program you desire to pursue.

Online Students Ought to Know:

8.   that **you decide during the week when to access your online course in asynchronous learning.** Most online courses are entirely asynchronous or at least the major portions of the online course are asynchronous. Asynchronous means that you do not have to be at a computer at a specific time. In other words you can participate and interact in your online course without the simultaneous interaction and exchange

of your student peers and instructor. Usually asynchronous courses do require you to come in weekly to post responses to discussion or message boards, submit assignments, and basically contribute to the course. You, the online student, determine the days and times in which you will engage your online course. Beware! Online courses are not self-paced. Be ready to do weekly work and make weekly contributions.

Online Students Ought to Know:

9.   that **some online courses require synchronous activities**. Oh, my goodness . . . another $50 dollar word! Synchronous means communication in which interaction between participants is simultaneous. This means that you, the online student, will be required to be at a computer at a specific time. The majority of synchronous learning occurs via Live Chats or seminars in which you, your student peers and instructor engage in thought exchange. Some of the newer technologies also

allow for interactive Whiteboard, streaming audio, and Powerpoint presentations. Please take note that these Chats are not about just building an online course connection or community, but are learning events. Therefore, it is very important that you do some advanced reading and studying to be prepared for these live events. Many online instructors will grade you on your preparedness, participation, and interactivity.

Online Students Ought to Know:

10. that **your local time may not be the same as your instructor's local time**. This is very important for those live synchronous events and good to understand when taking an online course. So now you are learning all about distance education, a specific courseware, your course content, and time zones. Well, to make it easy on yourself, just open up your phone book and flip through the front. There is usually a map of the USA

and the time zones that display the time differences. Don't forget the annual time changes. In the Spring you spring forward an hour and in the Fall you fall back an hour. This applies in most of the USA unless you live in Arizona, Native American reservations, and some local areas. If you get desperate to get it all figured out and are in a rush . . . call a telephone operator.

Online Students Ought to Know:

11. that **an online course may appear more expensive than a traditional course until you add up all your costs**. Think about it! You are an online student. Do you have to drive to class? How much are gas money and car expenses? How much time does it take you to get to your college? Do you have to dress up for class? How about childcare? Just think about all the time and expenses you expend for a traditional F2F

course that are not necessary in an online course. Some colleges do charge more for their online courses. This is largely due to the technology and the maintaining of online instructors. However, as more and more colleges start offering online courses and online degree programs it may be good to shop around for the best value.

Online Students Ought to Know:

12. that **financial aid is available in most instances just like it is for traditional F2F courses.** The opportunity to pursue grants and scholarships and have them apply to online courses is available. The same holds true for loans and any type of financial aid as long as you are attending an accredited institution. So, when it comes to any form of financial aid, you ought not to be discriminated against because you are an online student. Here are some sources to help you in your search for financial aid:

FinAid http://www.finaid.org/
Financial Aide Resource Center http://www.theoldschool.org/
The Student Guide: Financial Aide from the U.S. Department of
Education 2002-2003
http://www.ed.gov/prog_info/SFA/StudentGuide/2002-3/index.html

Online Students Ought to Know:

13. that **your grade for an online course is not identified on your official transcript any differently than your grades for traditional courses**. Good News! All courses you take with a college are listed on your transcript and NOT identified as to whether the course was a traditional F2F course or an online course. This is especially true of historically traditional colleges, which are creating courses and degree programs online. They cannot label a course on your transcript as being an online course. This ensures and underscores the value of your online course and degree program. So, your official transcript will not show that a course was delivered online or F2F.

Online Students Ought to Know:

14. that **most online courses contain all your course information up front at the beginning of the course.** What does this mean to you, the online student? It means you get to see your course for the whole semester or quarter up front: syllabus, assignments, requirements, lessons, supporting documents, website links, etc. This is a radical departure from the majority of traditional courses where the course comes to you in increments as it progresses. Most courseware allows course developers to build the course as a "one stop shop" for the online learner.

Online Students Ought to Know:

15. that **your online course has specific dates for early withdrawal or drop from a course, guidelines for incompletes, and the possibility of auditing**. Ultimately, you are responsible for your education and, therefore, it is very important that you keep track of your college's dates for dropping or withdrawing from a course. You need to know the date by which you can drop a course and get back your money. Please realize that after a certain date you will be liable for the cost of the course and will not have any money returned. Another important date is the last date for you to get a Withdraw

(W) so you can maintain your GPA. All these important dates, along with "incomplete" criteria are just the same for the traditional F2F course. Usually, for an Incomplete (I) you have to complete at least 75% of the course and then agree on an Incomplete Contract with your instructor. Some online courses are also available for audit. Please check with the instructor for audit permission. Do not assume that all online instructors accommodate students who want to audit their online course. Bottom line: If you have any questions, please contact Registration.

Online Students Ought to Know:

16. that **you will meet many people from diverse places, backgrounds, and experiences in an online course.** The online course environment is unique, especially in the student make-up. One of the things that make online learning very interesting and enjoyable is the diversity of online students that will be with you in your course. Many online courses have students from all over the United States and other countries from all corners of the globe. The diversity of students in terms of different places, cultures, ethnicities, religions, races, genders, and ages will enhance your overall online learning experience.

E-mail Chat
Barb: Louis, what are you doing tonight in Miami after you finish your online homework? It's snowing here in Vermont and we're going snow boarding. Maybe I'll test Professor Simon's velocity theory versus resistance.
Louis: Great idea! We're going sailing. Let's run two tests and compare notes.

Online Students Ought to Know:

17. that **you will learn many new words and phrases that are special to online learning.** Online learning is a new world and brings with it a new language. It is very important that as you delve into your online course and the phenomenon of online learning that you begin to acquire an understanding and knowledge of new terms and phrases. There are

many online education glossaries to help you. Please refer to the glossary in the back for an appendix of online words and phrases. Here are some online learning glossaries to refer to:

Distance Education Glossary
http://www.utexas.edu/cc/cit/de/deprimer/glossary.html
Distance Learning Glossary
http://www.wested.org/tie/dlrn/course/glossary.html

Online Students Ought to Know:

18. that you may have **special virtual guests attend and participate in your online course**. One of the most intriguing aspects of an online course is the possibility that your course instructor may invite guests to attend, participate, and interact with you and your fellow students in the course. Some online course instructors bring in periodic guests; such as, textbook authors, subject matter experts, learning support specialists, college administrators, and other guests to interact with their students.

Online Students Ought to Know:

19. that your **online course software (Blackboard, WebCT, eCollege, Desire2Learn, etc.) will require a learning curve**. So true! Plan on putting in some extra time to become comfortable with the courseware your online course utilizes. Attend a courseware orientation if your college provides one. If not, most coursewares that are used by colleges have a homepage with tutorials. Regardless it is very important that you take the time to familiarize yourself with the courseware. Learn what all the tabs and buttons do and most importantly refer to the Help button in the courseware and get familiar with its contents. You need to learn how to navigate throughout the

entire online course to see how all its parts and parcels function and operate. Knowing how to navigate an online course empowers you—the online student!

"The winds and the waves are always on the side of the ablest navigators." - Edward Gibbon, 1737-1794.

Blackboard http://blackboard.com/
eCollege http://ecollege.com/
WebCT http://webct.com

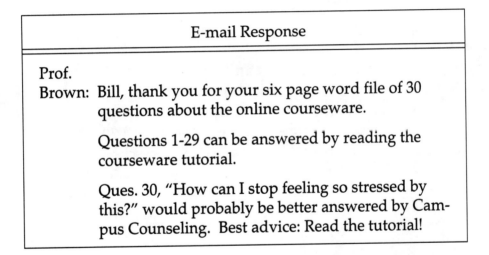

E-mail Response

Prof.
Brown: Bill, thank you for your six page word file of 30 questions about the online courseware.

Questions 1-29 can be answered by reading the courseware tutorial.

Ques. 30, "How can I stop feeling so stressed by this?" would probably be better answered by Campus Counseling. Best advice: Read the tutorial!

Online Students Ought to Know:

20. that your **online courses and online degree program are of great value**. Pursuing your education and completing a degree will increase your quality of life. The Distance Education and Training Council conducted a survey of 1,300 distance learning graduates from 21 accredited online schools and reported that 54% of them received an increase in pay due to their online degree. Fifty-percent of the graduates received a job promotion or had a career change. The value of education is with-

out question. Being able to take online courses or pursue an online degree enables you to stay in your locale and keep working as you move towards your academic goals.

The Distance Education and Training Council http://www.detc.org/

2 Online Access

Online Students Ought to Know:

21. that **you can search for specific accredited online programs or online courses offered by many different academic institutions**. The growth of online courses and online degree programs has brought about a competitive educational market, whereby you can search for those courses or degree programs that fit your lifestyle and career goals. Check the following websites for online courses and degree programs.

eLearners.Com http://www.elearners.com/search/courses.asp
Online Course Directory http://www.aln.org/coursedirectory/
TeleCampus Online Course Directory http://www.telecampus.edu

Online Students Ought to Know:

22. that **any course that you contemplate taking online for credit at an institution other than the one in which you are matriculated must be acceptable by your department head or academic advisor.** This is very important to check out prior to committing your finances and time. You want to make sure that a course is transferable into your degree program. Be aware that many colleges only allow a certain number of credits to be transferred into their degree programs. Always ask and make sure if a course is transferable. Better yet, get it in writing! It is your time, energy, and money— so always investigate. As the saying goes, "Better safe, than sorry!"

Online Students Ought to Know:

23. that there may be **specific academic counselors/advisors for online students**. Many colleges have specific people to give guidance for online students. Inquire if your college has specific academic counselors and/or advisors for online students. Find out all the pertinent contact information—address, phone number, and email. Make contact for guidance and to ensure you are making the right decisions about your online course or online degree program.

Online Students Ought to Know:

24. that **your college offers online registration and administrative support**. As a distance learner you will need all the help and support you can get. Collect all the contact information and write it down! For easy reference also create a word document file for safekeeping with all your contact notes to include: names, addresses, phone numbers, and email addresses. Learn always to resource yourself.

Online Students Ought to Know:

25. that you will be **given a user name and a password when you register for your course**. A user name is the name that you will be using to access your course. The password will be a temporary one that is assigned to you when you register for a course. As soon as you can, change the temporary password to one that you want to use for your course. Good passwords should be easy to remember and hard to forget. A

password that is difficult for others to figure out contains both letters and numbers. Since you might forget your course password especially since you may have different passwords for other Internet sites, write it down and keep it in a safe place. Do not share your username and password with anyone. They are your special code words to access and to work in your online course.

Online Students Ought to Know:

26. that **you are responsible to access your online course**. Although you are free to access your online course anytime day or night and although you are not required to be in a certain classroom at specified times during the week, you still need to schedule time to access your online course so that you can read course announcements, your instructor's lecture notes and assignment directions, and where you will take quizzes and exams. On the bright side, you do it on your schedule.

Online Students Ought to Know:

27. that **access to an online course may depend not only on the browser that you use but also on the version of the browser that you have**. A browser like Internet Explorer or Netscape, allows you to find, load, and view your course on the Internet. The directions for accessing your online course may specify not only what browsers you can use but also what version of these browsers are recommended. Be sure to find out what browsers and what versions of them that your college requires you to use in accessing your online course. If you have any browser problems, immediately contact your campus online administrator or technology help desk. Be aware that America Online may be a problem at your institution to access your online course.

3 Online Preparation

Online Students Ought to Know:

28. that **it is crucial to take a pre-assessment for online learning to ensure you are ready for the distance learning environment**. Are you ready for some online learning? Online learning is not for every student. So, the question is . . . do you have the right stuff? Along with being a self-motivated, self-disciplined student with superb time management skills, there are three major areas you need to have a pretty good handle on: a good, up to date working computer, basic computer skills, and a true understanding of what distance education is all about. Following are some pre-assessments to help

Online Students Ought to Know:

you measure if you are ready to jump into the online learning environment:

Cochise College Readiness Assessment
http://www.cochise.edu/assessment/register.cfm
DeAnza College Distance Learning Questionnaire
http://distance.deanza.fhda.edu/DLCQuestionnaire.shtml

Online Students Ought to Know:

29. that **an orientation to online learning is important**. Many colleges and their online campuses are providing orientations for beginning online learners. Some of these orientations are provided online and via the courseware (Blackboard, WebCT, eCollege, and others) you will be using for your online course. Some orientations are F2F in computer rooms to help the student become familiar with the courseware and some of the skills

necessary to succeed. Some students may need to complete an online learner orientation course. More and more colleges are beginning to offer such orientation courses for online learning. Bottom line: An orientation for the courseware your college uses and an orientation focusing on the unique and challenging world of online education will gear you up for success.

Online Students Ought to Know:

30. that **to be an online student you must be a moti-vated self-learner**. If there is a cornerstone to success as an online learner . . . it is here! You must be self-motivated! You are the one that has to turn on your computer and commit time to your online course. Try to find ways to motivate yourself, like small rewards for putting in a couple of hours here and there, and when completed a bigger self-award. Put some motivational quotes around your computer or a list of your academic and life goals. Following is a good motivational quote that you can use:

"Lose this day loitering - 'twill be the same story tomorrow and the next more dilatory. Then indecision brings its own delays, and days are lost lamenting over lost days. Are you in earnest? What you dream to do or think you can do, only begin it. Then the mind grows heated. Begin it, and work will be completed." - Goethe, 1749-1832

Online Students Ought to Know:

31. that **your computer meets the hardware and software configuration standards set by your college**. Do you want to set off on the right foot as an online learner? Well, this can make life much easier or very difficult. Most online campuses are going to post a typical profile for the hardware configuration you are going to need and that will be required for you to function with the online course successfully. Some colleges will require specific software for you to operate as a 100% up and ready online learner. Ask someone or send out email if you cannot locate the hardware and software configuration for your online course.

Online Students Ought to Know:

32. that **you must be computer literate**. There are degrees or levels of computer literacy. It is imperative that you have some basic computer skills and cannot only maneuver around the computer, but also the Internet. Many colleges offer a computer familiarization course and there are courses that do it all: basic computer skills, Internet skills, and distance education familiarization. An honest self-assessment is best. If you do not know much about the computer other than turning it on, and really do not understand the Internet, then perhaps a familiarization course is best for you. Please check out your college or the online campus for specific course offerings.

Online Students Ought to Know:

33. that **you must have an email address to communi-cate in an online course**. Yes, an email address is most essential for you to be an online learner. You will have an email account if you are paying for monthly Internet service with a national or local Internet provider. You can also create an email account with many free email services like Netscape.net, Hotmail.com, or Yahoo.com. Many colleges provide free email

addresses to their students. Inquire with the online campus of your college to see if it will provide you with an email address and service. It is strongly advised that you do not change your email address in the middle of an online course. If you do change your email address, most courseware will allow you to edit your profile and email address.

Online Students Ought to Know:

34. that **you must have a copy of the course text on hand for your first week of class**. Be a proactive online student! Most colleges and/or online campuses publish an online list of textbooks for all online courses. Please attempt to get your textbook as early as possible and do not wait until the 11th hour! Remember as an online learner you can ill afford to get behind!! Access online bookstores for new and used textbooks and shop around for the best buy. Following are some websites for online bookstores selling new and used textbooks.

Amazon. Com http://www.amazon.com
Barnes and Noble. Com http://barnesandnoble.com/
BigWords.Com http://www.bigwords.com/
BookFinder.Com http://www.bookfinder.com
eCampus.Com http://www.ecampus.com
Powell's Bookstore http://www.powells.com
Textbookx.Com http://www.textbookx.com
VarsityBooks.Com http://www.varsitybooks.com

Online Students Ought to Know:

35. that **your textbook may have a companion website or CD-ROM with additional resources and information**. Your first task when you get the textbook for your online course is to familiarize yourself with the text. Many publishers create a companion website for a text which contains many other helpful sources. Publishers are also creating major generic discipline sites, which can be extremely helpful. So, check out your text. If your text comes with a CD-ROM you have a wealth of resources at your fingertips. Explore the CD-ROM to see what it contains immediately. These additional text supported sources can save you a great deal of time and energy. Scout 'em out!

Online Students Ought to Know:

36. that **you need to schedule 9 to 12 hours for weekly course work in each three-credit online course in which you are enrolled**. Well, stop and think about! The traditional F2F course for a semester or quarter usually meets 3 or 4 hours a week. Meeting in a classroom does not count the time to read, study, and prepare for class. And then there is the time to spend on assignments, requirements, projects, and writing of research papers. The truly successful online students who are in the "A" zone are reporting an investment of a minimum of 9-12 hours a week per online course.

Online Students Ought to Know:

37. that **an online course syllabus is there to be read**. Okay! It might be a great labor, but it could also save your bacon and help you to be a successful online student. Read the syllabus! Read the syllabus, again. If something in the syllabus needs clarification, email the instructor. The syllabus is the foundation of the course. You need to read, comprehend, and follow it in detail. Most online courses have the syllabus right there for you to read and even print out. You are encouraged to print out the syllabus so you can read it and refer to it off-line. Oh, yeah, one last thing—read the syllabus!

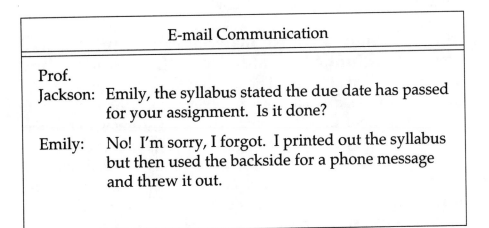

E-mail Communication

Prof.
Jackson: Emily, the syllabus stated the due date has passed
for your assignment. Is it done?

Emily: No! I'm sorry, I forgot. I printed out the syllabus
but then used the backside for a phone message
and threw it out.

Online Students Ought to Know:

38. that **all online course material can be printed and stored in a binder or folder for offline reading and work**. Oh, what a beautiful tie into our last point regarding the syllabus. Create a notebook or special folder for each online course. Print out those materials you want to refer to off-line: syllabus, course documents, assignments, examples, etc. This really beats sitting in front of a computer endlessly. With the printed out course materials you can go off-line and sit somewhere else to read, study, and write. Give your neck, back, and eyes a break —create a course notebook for your online course to work off-line!

Online Students Ought to Know:

39. that **you need to schedule the times in your calendar to work on your online course**. This is a must! If you do not have some sort of calendar book (Day Timer, Day Scheduler, etc.) it is time to purchase one! There are also many varieties of electronic PIMS (Personal Information Management System) like Microsoft Outlook, etc. The important thing is to schedule your course into your calendar by whatever method you choose. Be deliberate! Schedule in all those due dates, but more

importantly those times which you will commit to be in front of the computer and involved in your online course. As a good rule you want to do this prior to beginning your course. Then double-check it every Sunday night for the coming week. Note: Be especially careful if synchronous discussions are scheduled. Not being a participant is probably worse than missing a class. You will be noticed.

Online Students Ought to Know:

40. that **you need to create a special diskette or zip drive for online course organization**. Setting up your online course with strong and specific organization determines your success. Failure to organize will lead to confusion, frustration, and ultimately a bad grade or withdrawal from the course. So, as the course begins you need to create and label a special diskette for each course. Create a word document to maintain all of your course notes like the course url, username, password,

etc. Use the diskette to put your work on and save assignments and anything else you think is worthy for effective course management. It doesn't hurt to have a special course folder on your hard drive in your My Documents folder, but back it up on your diskette or a zip drive if you have one. You can put all your files within the course folders you create. Bottom line: Organize and back-up all your work, all the time!

Online Students Ought to Know:

41. that **you need some basic Internet searching skills and sources**. You are taking an online course! You need to become an Internet master, an Internet web warrior! You will become a more successful online student the more empowered you become in your ability to search quickly and effectively on the Internet. You need to create a course folder in your Bookmarks or Favorites to save all those great websites that will help you with assignments and papers. Just knowing a few search engines is not enough. You must develop the capacity to narrow searches and stay on task when researching on the Internet. Following are some sources for you.

AllTheWeb.Com http://www.alltheweb.com
Dogpile Multi-Search Engine http://www.dogpile.com
Google.Com http://www.google.com
Merlot.Org http://www.merlot.org
Northern Light http://www.northernlight.com
RDN Virtual Training Suite http://www.vts.rdn.ac.uk/
SearchEngineWatch.Com http://searchenginewatch.com/
Yahoo! Advanced Web Search
http://search.yahoo.com/search/options

Basch, R. and Bates, M. E. (2000). *Researching online for dummies*, 2nd Edition. Foster City, CA: IDG Books Worldwide, Inc. ISBN 0-7645-0546-7. Comes with CD-ROM.

Schlein, A. M. (2002). *Find it online: The complete guide to online research*, 3rd Edition. Tempe, AZ: Facts On Demand Press. ISBN 1-889150-29-0.

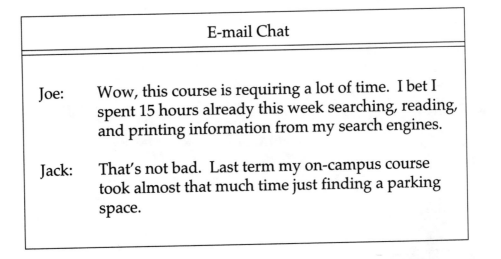

E-mail Chat

Joe: Wow, this course is requiring a lot of time. I bet I spent 15 hours already this week searching, reading, and printing information from my search engines.

Jack: That's not bad. Last term my on-campus course took almost that much time just finding a parking space.

4 Online Communications

Online Students Ought to Know:

42. that **your online course contains many tools and ways in which to communicate with your fellow online students and instructor.** You are really never alone in an online course! Online courses are not self-paced and independent like correspondence courses. While the majority of online learning is independent, you will have the opportunity to communicate with your student peers and instructor. Communicating via email is common today, and via some courseware you

may have an internal email system for the course or your college may provide an email system. Many courses use discussion boards for interactivity, reflections on readings, and postings of assignments. Many types of courseware (Blackboard, WebCT, Desire2Learn and eCollege) also allow for document exchange. Some courses will have synchronous communication activities utilizing Virtual Classroom, Chats, and Whiteboard. Bottom line: You will be in constant contact with the members of your course.

Online Students Ought to Know:

43. that **only you, your fellow online students, and your instructor will have access to your work in the course**. Your online course is not open for the world to view. Most colleges will only allow paying students into an online course and you will be provided a username and password. Some courseware allows you to create or edit your profile so that you can change your username and password. It is very important

that you know how to access your course. So, write down and save all information on how to access your course, including your username and password. Protect your username and password! Do not share your username and password with anyone. This ensures that the work submitted is yours and not someone else's. Also, sharing your username and password might be in violation of your college's Student Code of Conduct.

Online Students Ought to Know:

44. that **your course email does not allow spam**. Good news in these days of spam overload! Your college does not sell or exchange your email address to businesses or email profiteers. Most online courses are private or "closed" and that means only your student peers and instructor have access to your email. Some online course etiquette is also necessary here. Namely, that all members—students and instructors—stay on the learn-

ing task. This is not the opportunity to push any kind of business, product, or service. If you see anyone violating online course email protocol, report him or her immediately to your instructor or online campus administrator. Be advised that the more you give out your email to companies and the variety of websites will greatly increase spam traffic.

Online Students Ought to Know:

45. that **you may be requested to create a homepage.** The majority of online courses utilize a number of ways and means to build a connected learning community. This is important so that online students realize they are not alone, but a vital part of a group of online learners who have come together in cyberspace. Perhaps one thing you will be required to do, or enabled to do via some courseware, is build your own homepage. The good news is that it is simple and you don't have to be a certified computer geek to do so. Most of these types of homepages are just a simple profile where you infuse some personal information and maybe a photo if you desire. Bottom line: Building a homepage helps to build a stronger sense of community in your online course.

Online Students Ought to Know:

46. that **you need to learn how to use discussion boards and how to thread correctly in discussion boards**. For many online courses the discussion boards are the very heart and soul of the online course. This is the place for thought exchange, reading reflections, and interactivity on the subject. So, it is very important that you take the time to learn and master how the discussion board works and how to post your comments/responses correctly. Most discussions are 'threaded' or

tiered as they develop. So to respond to the originator of the thread you must follow it up to the top and click there to respond to them. As a rule always ask yourself. "To whom do I want to respond?" Then ensure that is indeed to whom you are responding. Please refer to the courseware "Help" button to learn this. Bottom line: Practice! Practice! Practice! Practice until you get it right and get in the rhythm.

Online Students Ought to Know:

47. that **your participation and interactivity are vital to your success**. Pretty crucial to your online course success is your participation and interactivity in the course. There are some key reasons for this: attendance and grading. Your weekly "appearance" in the online course validates attendance. So be involved and participate to validate your attendance. Since participation and interactivity play a vital role in many online courses you will find that it is a percentage of your final grade. Beware that you may lose points by not participating and interacting with your fellow online students. Be involved! Contribute and participate in your online learning experience.

Online Students Ought to Know:

48. that **most online courses have space allotted to meet and socialize with your fellow students**. Many online educators are developing into their online courses a place for "students only." Most of these opportunities will come via the discussion board area and might be called "Arena of Discussion," "Watercooler," "Cyber Student Union," "All Around The Watch Tower," etc. This becomes a place for students to engage one another with questions, discussion, help, and clarification on course assignments. Some online courses will allow for student lead live chats. This creates a place and opportunity for online students to connect and build an online course community.

Online Students Ought to Know:

49. that **only you can see your grades in the online course gradebook**. The online course gradebook is something very unique to online learning. If you have a proactive online instructor who maintains the gradebook weekly, you will know constantly where you are grade-wise in the course. This does not happen as often in traditional F2F courses. Once the grades are posted in the online gradebook, only you can see **your** scores. The online gradebook is a vital tool for any online course because it readily helps to connect the student and the instructor and keeps students on task.

Online Students Ought to Know:

50. that **your email organization is vital to your online course success**. This is another one of those very important areas for your online course success. As your course begins you ought to create a labeled course folder in your email manager to save important emails. You could even categorize your emails by the week of the course. Many online instructors send out weekly email with a great deal of information in them. Read and Save! If there are any emails with vital information—save!

Online Students Ought to Know:

51. that **an email message is different from face-to-face communication**. Email communication is the primary means of communication between online students and their course instructor and student peers. You need to learn and master some basics in email etiquette and protocol since effective communication is critical in any endeavor or enterprise. Effective email communication is an art and takes some discipline. Emailing others is not a time to be lazy or sloppy in your writ-

ing. Bottom line: Be professional.

Below are some resources to awaken you to the vital area of email etiquette:

Yale University Library - Email Etiquette
http://www.library.yale.edu/training/netiquette/
Email Etiquette - http://www.emailreplies.com/

Online Students Ought to Know:

52. that **you need to fill out the subject line correctly on all your email communications**. Another sign of the lazy student is the student who does not put anything in the SUBJECT line of an email or information that does not help the online instructor. You need to fill out the SUBJECT line of every email with pertinent information that will help your instructor identify you. Use the SUBJECT line to identify yourself and the body of the email message to speak to your question, concern, or problem. The key information that needs to be identified in the

SUBJECT line is college, course, and your name. Let's say you are taking an Introduction to Sociology (SOC101) course at the Community College of Southern Nevada. The correct way to fill out the SUBJECT line would be - CCSN/SOC101/YourLastName. And most importantly sign your full name at the end of every email. Online instructors do not memorize email addresses. Be professional.

Online Students Ought to Know:

53. that **you ought to draft your email and discussion board messages in MSWord**. Why? Well, most email programs will check your spelling if you willfully run the spell check, but will not check basic grammar. Discussion Boards as a rule do not have spelling or grammar checks. Your written communication is a reflection of you. Make a practice of drafting your written communications in MSWord to catch basic misspellings and grammar problems. Once it looks clean and presentable, copy and paste it into your email to send. Be professional.

Online Students Ought to Know:

54. that **any email you write when you are angry or upset with the course, your instructor, or your fellow students ought to be placed in your draft folder**. Even with the best of intentions, misunderstandings are likely to occur in almost any type of communication. It is possible to repair glitches in a face-to-face dialog or even a telephone conversation before any lasting damage occurs. However, email does not offer the benefit of these signals for email users. So, it is best to use the draft folder that is in your email management system, which

can help reduce misunderstandings and other communication challenges that occur when emotional emails are sent out immediately. So, if you find yourself getting ready to send off an email full of emotion, pause and put it in your email draft folder for a day. Then come back and revisit the email. Edit the email and then send it if you feel it is necessary. Students find that when they do this, 9 out of 10 times they just delete the email and move on. Bottom line: Be professional.

Online Students Ought to Know:

55. that **many online courses have an internal email system**. This is worthy to check out and investigate whether your courseware or college has its own email system. This helps to free up your own email account and email management. Most of these internal courseware or college systems allow you to receive, send, and manage your emails within the online course you are taking. These internal email systems have most of the tools of any email management system. If you are taking multiple courses you can create different labeled folders for each course to maintain and manage your email.

Online Students Ought to Know:

56. that **most communication between you and your instructor will be asynchronous**. The term asynchronous means that communication in the course will occur at different times. In online education, most of your communication will occur via discussion boards where you will post a message and then your instructor or other students will respond to that message at a later time. So it is important to realize that you may not get an immediate response on your posting. However, most online courses are set up with weekly assignments, requirements, and interactivity so your instructor will respond to you or the class within a week.

Online Students Ought to Know:

57. that **your online instructor may not reply immediately to your question or comment**. This ties in with the previous point and it is important for online students to realize that their online instructor has many courses and many students. Most online instructors will do their utmost to reply to email with 24-48 hours. For discussion boards and other assignments it is important to be patient and wait for response a good full week after the class due date. Keep working on the online course and assignments while you are waiting for response from your instructor.

Online Discussion Board

Linda: Thanks all! I appreciate all your responses to my question to Dr. Yates. It's great getting so much help. Do you think that's what Dr. Yates planned for us to do?

Dr.
Yates: Yup!

5 Online Learning and Study Skills & Strategies

Online Students Ought to Know:

58. that **you need to commit time both to access your course and for off-line reading and writing**. Most students who drop out of online courses, say that there is not enough time to do the course work. These students are mostly ones who have not invested their time in learning about time management. A good source to learn about time management is an inexpensive paperback entitled *How to Get Control of Your Time and Your Life* by Alan Lakein. To shop online for this book refer to #34.

Making time on your weekly personal schedule to do the reading, writing, exam preparation, and group work for your online course is critical to your success. Although you can study-read your assignments and write your course papers away from the computer, you still need to schedule time to access your course daily, to read announcements, and to respond to fellow students' discussion board assignments. You will also need to set aside blocks of time to do long term assignments like annotated bibliographies and research papers. Some instructors indicate that students need to schedule at least 9 to 12 hours weekly for every online course that they are taking if they expect to do well in the course and get good grades.

Online Students Ought to Know:

59. that **most of your learning will be done through reading**. Reading is important in all your courses both traditional and online. However, in online courses, reading becomes the only way that you will be getting course information since most online courses do not use audio as part of their instruction. If you think that you need to improve your reading skills, consider taking a campus course in reading, getting access to reading improvement software, spending time on the Internet collecting web pages that focus on reading skills, or going to

Amazon.com for some titles that may help you improve your reading. Use search terms like "reading skills," or "reading strategies." to find improvement materials.

Suggestions for Improving Reading Speed
http://www.ucc.vt.edu/stdysk/suggest.html
How to Improve Reading Comprehension
http://www.marin.cc.ca.us/~don/Study/7read.html

Online Students Ought to Know:

60. that **study-reading is a crucial skill**. Almost every task that you will be assigned to complete in an online course involves reading whether it is the required course textbook, articles on reserve in an electronic library, or articles on the Internet. Most online courses do not have audio lectures so that your success in an online course is strongly dependent on your reading skills. You will have much reading to do both in your required text and in reading assignments on the Internet. Much of the reading that you will be required to do will involve your using the information from your reading to answer instructor assigned questions and to integrate it in your research papers.

This study-reading is different from reading for pleasure. It is a more active form of reading that will help you to find main ideas and supporting details as well as to remember them. Study-reading is best done using a recommended procedure like SQ3R (Survey, Question, Read, Recite, Review). For students who learn visually, a mapping system might be preferred. You can find specific directions for study-reading methods in most how-to-study books and on the Internet.

How Can I Organize My Textbook Reading? Or Unraveling The Textbook Maze
http://www.sla.purdue.edu/studentserv/learningcenter/handouts/txtvid94.htm
Critical Reading Strategies http://mind.phil.vt.edu/www/1204crs.html

---

Online Students Ought to Know:

61. that **online course assignments require a combination of reading and writing skills**. Just as reading assumes a greater role in online courses than in most traditional courses, writing also becomes more important. In addition to writing research papers as you do in traditional courses, you will be writing many emails and responding weekly to reading questions with essay answers. Much of your writing will focus on your response or reaction to writing whether it is a fellow student's email or a discussion board response to an essay question.

Online Students Ought to Know:

62. that **you need to plan your online course work and follow your plan**. It cannot be overemphasized that you must plan your online time. Even if it is not the same time every week, you need to schedule it on your calendar. You might label your online time as online access time, study time, and assignment time. Scheduling time for these three is especially critical in the first couple of weeks of your online course and even more critical if you have never taken an online course before. Remem-

ber that generally a three-unit online course requires at least 9 to 12 hours of viewing and study time. In addition, you will need to budget time for major written assignments. If you have any difficulty in planning your time, email your instructor for assistance.

How to Manage Time and Set Priorities:
http://www.marin.cc.ca.us/~don/Study/5time.html

Online Students Ought to Know:

63. that **you need to keep track of your assignments and complete them on time.** Part of your time management plan is to complete your assignments when they are due. In your course binder, keep a list of all assignments along with their due dates. Refer to this list weekly. Print out instructions for each assignment and then check them off as they are completed. Do not get behind in your assignments. Meet your assignment deadlines. Some instructors will penalize you if you do not turn in your assignments on their due dates.

Online Students Ought to Know:

64. that **you follow directions for all your course assignments**. Of all the advice that both online instructors and students mention frequently, the most important relates to an instructor's directions for course assignments. This advice can be summed up in one statement: *Find, read, and follow directions.* You might want to print this statement in large letters and post it next to your monitor and also in your course binder. It is very important and will make a difference in your course grade.

Following Directions
http://www.apurnell.com/images/FOLLOWING%20DIRECTIONS.htm

Online Students Ought to Know:

65. that **currently available on the Internet are thousands of web pages that may be helpful**. This wealth of available Internet material is not only a blessing but also a challenge. Hopefully, your online course instructor has narrowed down your choices with some direction and advice in your course information. Your instructor may even recommend certain search engines that are useful for your course assignments. If your instructor has not made any recommendations, you may want to look at Alta Vista, Excite, Google, or Yahoo. You may already

have a link to one or more search engines on the home page of your Internet Service Provider (ISP). Whichever search engine you choose to use, you will be using a keyword or phrase to find what you are looking for. As you enter your search words or phrases, be sure that you have spelled them correctly. A search engine looks for words that you have entered not for words that you intended to enter. If you need assistance with Internet searching, see a college or local librarian.

Online Students Ought to Know:

66. that **help with reading and study skills may be available on campus**. Find out if your campus offers any reading or study skills classes that you can take to improve your reading and study skills. You might also check to see if you can visit a campus reading center or study skills center for assistance. Sometimes a center will make available reading software that you can use to improve your reading skills.

Online Students Ought to Know:

67. that **you can get practical help for online learning and study problems in how-to-study books**. You know that there are hundreds of how-to-study books available commercially. Even if you are a good student and feel confident that you have great study strategies, you may want to buy a how-to-study book and keep it handy for those times when you have a question about a particular study strategy. How-to-study books are also available on loan from a campus or local library.

Online Students Ought to Know:

68. that **you may be able to visit a campus learning support center, a math, writing, or tutorial center for assistance with your course work**. Some online students want face-to-face contact with a learning skills specialist, a math tutor, a writing tutor, or a subject matter tutor. If you are one of those students, find out if there is a learning center, a writing center, a math center, or tutor center at a nearby college. Many college learning assistance centers will provide services to non-campus students although some centers may charge a fee for these services.

Online Students Ought to Know:

69. that **help with math, both basic and advanced, may be found on the Internet**. If you are not taking your online course on your campus where you can use tutors for math assistance, you can still get help on the Internet. Use a search engine and type in its search box a keyword or phrase like algebra, geometry, and calculus. Your search will yield web sites that help you learn theorems, solve problems, and even lead you to some tutor web sites on which you can ask math questions and

get answers back to your email address. Remember also that you can sometimes get face to face help at a local college or university by going to its learning support center, tutoring center, or math lab.

Professor Freedman's Math Help at http://www.mathpower.com/
Western Nebraska Community College Math Study Tips
http://hannibal.wncc.cc.ne.us/mathcenter/mathtips/index.html

Online Students Ought to Know:

70. that **help with your writing is available online**. Many colleges that offer online courses or degrees have developed their own online writing centers. Modeled after Purdue University's famous OWL (Online Writing Center), these online campus OWLS offer web pages that can help you with grammar, punctuation, writing style, essay and research papers. Some OWLS have email and chat available. Through an email exchange or a synchronous chat feature, you can get personal help with

almost any writing problem that you will encounter in your course work.

Anthony Hughes' Online English Grammar
http://www.edufind.com/english/grammar/
Purdue University's Online Writing Lab   http://owl.english.purdue.edu/
The Writing Center at the University of Wisconsin-Madison
http://www.wisc.edu/writing/

Online Students Ought to Know:

71. that **additional help with your writing may be found in writing manuals and grammar handbooks.** Most good writers keep a grammar or style manual available for use when they have a writing problem. You can get one at almost any bookstore. One book we would recommend is Hult, C.A. and Huckin, T.N. (2002). *The New Century Handbook*, 2nd Edition. New York, NY: Pearson/Longman. ISBN 0205329705. Comes with a CD-Rom and a great companion website http://www.ablongman.com/hult.

Online Students Ought to Know:

72. that **help with learning and study skills is available on the Internet**. Like help with reading, math, and writing, you can find loads of Internet sites that offer learning and study skills tips and tutorials. Just type in a term like "time management," "study environment," "textbook reading," "note taking," "test taking," or "writing a term paper" and you will get many useful tips that you can use to improve your learning and studying. Rather than spending a lot of time on the Internet

OUACHITA TECHNICAL COLLEGE

reading these tips, print them and place them in a "Help" section of your course binder for use when you need them.

Study Guides and Strategies Webliography at
http://www.iss.stthomas.edu/studyguides/
Chemeketa CC Study Skills Resources
http://www.howtostudy.org/resources.htm

Online Students Ought to Know:

73. that **study groups can be helpful for course success**. Active learning occurs in a group where students question each other and comment on their fellow students' assignments. If your instructor does not place you in a study or project group, consider creating your own study group that can meet in a chat room or by email. Keep your group small with three to five in your group. For chats, set a time that is mutually agreeable to meet and chat. If students are in different time zones, keep that in mind when you set your chat times. Groups work best when someone is in charge to set a purpose for each meeting and to keep discussions on target. Being in a group can help you stay

interested in a course since group members tend to support each other.

Using Study Groups Effectively from the University of Dayton
http://academic.udayton.edu/aep/online/exams/study02.htm
Using study groups to increase learning
http://www.coun.uvic.ca/learn/program/hndouts/studygr.html
Online Teams http://www.learnntc.com/transition/teamwork.shtml

---

Online Students Ought to Know:

74. that **tutors may be available for most online courses**. At some time during your online course, you may find that you need someone to answer a question on your reading or writing assignment or to help you with a math or science problem. Look for tutors at your home institution, at a nearby college or university tutor center, or on the Internet at a college web site or from a commercial tutoring service.

Online Students Ought to Know:

75. that **your tests and exams will be completed online**. Online tests may be true/false, completion, matching, or essay type questions. Most tests can be taken when you decide to do so. Some tests, however, are scheduled on specific days and at specific times. Some tests also require you to take your test within a specified number of days and for a specific duration of time. For most tests your notes and textbook will be helpful.

Online Students Ought to Know:

76. that **you should initially type all text for course assignments with your word processor**. Instead of typing answers to reading questions directly in your courseware, write and edit them with your word processor. Before you copy any written assignment from your word processor document to your courseware, use its spell and grammar checker to ensure that your written assignments are error free when your instructor reads them. If you consistently misspell words or use unacceptable grammar, your instructor may not only downgrade your work but may require you to rewrite your assignment.

Online Students Ought to Know:

77. that **a spell checker does not always find spelling errors**. It does not, for example, alert you to words that sound alike so that if you spell "lye" for "lie," your spell checker will allow it even though you did not intend to use it. The preferred way to check spelling is to have a friend proof it for spelling. If most of your spelling mistakes are the result of keyboard accidents, reading your writing aloud will catch keyboard errors since many spelling errors are caused by misplaced fingering on the keyboard rather than on any misspelling.

Online Students Ought to Know:

78. that **for some courses you may be required to do some examinations at a computer under the watchful eyes of a proctor.** In some online courses, you will take tests on a nearby college campus where you must show a photo ID card before you take the test. Tests are an integral part of most courses whether they are quizzes, mid-terms, or finals. Most online testing is done through essay question on course readings or objective tests that may be true/false, multiple choice, or matching. In some courses, the final is not offered or taken online.

You may be required to take your final at a nearby college or at a commercial test center where you will take your test at a time mutually agreed upon by you and an assigned test proctor. Such tests may be timed tests. Although you may be assigned an open book test in which you may be allowed to use your course text and notes, most tests will be similar to your traditional classroom tests. Before you go to the location of your proctored test, be sure that you know what materials you may bring to the test site.

Online Students Ought to Know:

79. that **most of your online course study and assignments can be completed offline**. Remember that much of your course reading and study can be done off-line away from an Internet connected computer. You may be doing your written assignments on your desktop, laptop, or PDA. If you have made print copies of your courseware material and stored them in your course binder, you will be able to study anywhere that you consider appropriate for study.

Online Students Ought to Know:

80. that **the best answers to reading questions occur when you rewrite the question as the lead into your answer**. Students lose points on essay questions for answers that do not focus on what the instructor has asked for in his or her question. For example, a question that asks you to list and describe terms will get you few if any points if you only list the terms and do not describe them. This is also true if you are asked to contrast two ideas and you compare them in your answer.

How to read essays you must analyze
http://www.ucc.vt.edu/stdysk/essays.html

Online Students Ought to Know:

81. that **plagiarism is unethical**. Ted Frick, an Indiana University professor states that plagiarism occurs when a writer does not give credit to an author for the author's words or statements, either quoted or paraphrased. Plagiarism also includes the borrowing of facts, statistics, or illustrative material that is not common knowledge or the use of another person's ideas, opinions, or theories. Indiana University's "Code of Student Rights, Responsibilities, and Conduct, Part III, Student Misconduct, Academic Misconduct, " Retrieved October 9, 2002 from http://education.indiana.edu/~frick/plagiarism/index2.html.

Regardless whether plagiarism is unintentional or deliberate, you avoid it by giving credit to all your sources. Be aware that some online campuses are using software successfully to detect plagiarism. Be also aware that at some institutions plagiarism is grounds for dismissal.

What is Plagiarism? A Short Concept Lesson by Ted Frick, Indiana University. http://education.indiana.edu/~frick/plagiarism/

Online Students Ought to Know:

82. that **you may be required to send your assignments via email to your instructor or to a designated course drop box**. For most online assignments, you will be required to attach your work as a word document file either to an email or send it to a special section of your courseware where your instructor can read, comment on, and grade your assignment. With email, you attach your document. For some assignments, you send them to a Digital Drop Box. Follow your instructor's specific instructions and guidelines. Do not forget to give all pertinent information like your course name and your full name. Refer to #52.

Online Students Ought to Know:

83. how **to access journal databases for articles**. Throughout your online course, you will be required to find, read, and use material from online professional journals. Early in your course, locate any information that lists or discusses professional sources that you are required or recommended to use. This may be a list of external links to Internet sources. It may be an internal link to the Internet source directly from the instructor's directions for an assignment. If you have any difficulty in locating and accessing journal information, email your instructor or go to your campus library or local public library for assistance.

Online Students Ought to Know:

84. how **to distinguish websites that have academic credibility**. The Internet contains millions of web pages, many of which are written by persons with no academic background. Your instructor will most certainly demand that you use credible sources for any research that you do for the course. The information you find on a web site may be partially or totally unacceptable to your instructor, who will probably require you to document your sources in a format that indicates the address

of the web page on which you located the information and the date on which you retrieved it from that page.

Evaluating Internet Research Sources
http://www.virtualsalt.com/evalu8it.htm

Online Students Ought to Know:

85. how **to recognize specialized sources of Internet information**. The Internet has assigned special names to different types of information. These names are known as domains. Domains can be recognized by looking at the last two to four letters after the period in an Internet address. Some common domain names that you will be using in your online research are the following: "com," used by individuals, non-profits, and companies; "org," used by noncommercial organizations; "gov," used by U.S. government agencies; "mil," used by the U.S. military; and "edu," used by educational institutions. Domain names may be useful in determining the origin and the authenticity of Internet information.

Online Students Ought to Know:

86. that **you may be required to submit your written assignments in a specific document format**. Because of the limitations of some software and courseware, you may be required to send assignments to your instructor in a special word processing format. This may be as a Word document as a rich text file. In some courses, you may not send a word perfect file, Wordpad, Notepad, or a Lotus Notes file. You can, however,

send your written assignments as a rich text file. Remember that Word has a doc extension and Word Perfect a wps extension. The overwhelming majority of colleges and universities use the tools in Microsoft Office—Word, PowerPoint, Excel, Outlook, etc. Shop around for student and educational discounts.

6 Online Student Support

Online Students Ought to Know:

87. that **one of the best resources for help in an online course is a student with online experience**. Find an experienced online student to become your mentor. This can be a former student who was successful in your online course. It can be a friend who has had online experience especially in the courseware that you are using or in the very course that you are taking. Not only can you get help from your mentor face to face

but you can also get help communicating by email or even by telephone. You may even find a fellow student on your home campus or at a nearby college.

Advice from "Those who Know" on Taking Weber State U-Online Courses
http://wsuonline.weber.edu/studsupport/sucess_stud/advice.htm

Online Students Ought to Know:

88. that **no question that you ask an instructor is a dumb question**. Most online instructors indicate that students do not ask questions about course procedures or about their assignments. If the course instructor has a virtual faculty office within the course, post your question there. If your instructor has given you an email address or a telephone number that can be accessed, use it whenever you have a problem or a question on your assignments. Do not wait to ask your question. Of course, before you ask your question, be sure you have looked at the course material to see if the answer to your question is there. If

you feel embarrassed to ask your instructor a question, email a fellow student or your course mentor if you have one. Remember that your unasked question can cost you valuable course points.

Asking questions - in class and out!
http://www.chass.ncsu.edu/ccstm/scmh/questions.html
Do you never ask questions in class?
http://www.math.utah.edu/~alfeld/math/a22.html

Online Students Ought to Know:

89. whether **your college provides online students with special library connections, resources, and research assistance**. Since most of your online course assignments will require access to online resources, you will find that your course may have links to Internet resources already described in your course information or listed and linked in a course webliography (a list of web sites). Your instructor may also suggest Internet databases to which the library has subscribed that will be useful for your course. In addition, many course instructors have an arrangement with their college library to have specific book chap-

ters, monographs, and articles available to students for the duration of their course. These special materials are materials that are not in the Internet databases that the library has subscribed to but are copied in web format and placed in a special online reserve collection for your course. This collection is accessed on the Internet with a special user name and password that your instructor will describe in your course information. If you want face-to-face assistance from a librarian and you are far from your college library, remember that you can get help from your local public librarian.

Online Students Ought to Know:

90. whether **your college provides technical assistance**. Unless you are a super computer expert and an Internet guru, you will find that you will need some help to solve problems that occur as you work with your computer programs, your browser, or your courseware. If your college has a special web site or web pages dedicated to online courses, look there to see if it has a Help Desk that you can use. These help desks are publicized as 24/7 services that can be accessed either online or through email contact. Don't forget that technical help may be available also at your local library, a local college or university, or a local computer user group. In addition, find out if your institution offers a toll-free number for technical and courseware help.

Online Students Ought to Know:

91. whether **your college library, learning support center, and bookstore have a collection of books that focus on learning and study support for online students**. You will find many useful how-to-study books in a college library, community public library, a campus learning support center, and in a campus bookstore. Bookstores like Borders and Barnes & Noble also carry how-to-study books in their self-improvement section. At your campus library, look in its catalogue under the heading of "study skills," "online learning" or "distance education."

Online Students Ought to Know:

92. that **your online course may have a help desk available for courseware problems**. Good news for online students! More and more colleges with online programs are hosting help desks to assist students and to increase online student retention. Most of these help desks provide assistance with computer problems, access problems, and courseware problems. Most of the help desks build a collection of FAQ's (Frequently Asked Questions) with definitive, specific answers to help the online student. Some help desks go the extra mile and will assist with online learning skills and referrals to SME's (Subject Matter Experts). You are encouraged to write down or save the url and all the contact information of your Help Desk.

Online Students Ought to Know:

93. that **your online course may have an 800 toll free number available for assistance**. Again it is critical to inquire as to what your college's online program offers in the way of student support and services. Write down and save as a document file all the pertinent contact information, including the 800 number to the Help Desk or Online Campus office if your college provides such a service. Ensure that you have this information in your course folder and save the document of contact information on your course labeled diskette. Keep that diskette in your course folder.

Online Students Ought to Know:

94. that **most online courses have a virtual faculty office to which you can send your course questions anytime**. Most online faculty will have some set hours during which they will be online doing course work and checking email. Capture this information from the online course or syllabus. If the information isn't there, ask your online instructor if he/she keeps virtual office hours. Some online faculty will host definitive days and hours of virtual office times for synchronous communication or live chat.

Online Students Ought to Know:

95. how **to navigate through your online course**. It is very important for new online students to take some time to learn how their online course works. So investigate your course. Find out what all the buttons and tabs do and learn your way through the course and see what is available for you since often online courses have many resources and tools within the online course to make your learning easier and more enjoyable. Many online faculty develop their online courses to be a one-stop shop for you by providing all sorts of resources. So, initially it is very important to play the role of an adventurer and learn how your course works—what it provides and how it functions.

Online Students Ought to Know:

96. that **Student Manuals for Blackboard, WebCT, Desire2Learn, and eCollege are available online**. As stated earlier it is most critical to become familiar with the courseware of your online course. While this takes some additional time, it will be crucial to your success as an online student. Learning the courseware and all that is contained within the shell of your course will make your online learning easier and save you time in the long run. So, you are strongly encouraged to download and print the Student Study or Help Guide

that goes with your courseware. The Student Study / Help Guide will prove to be an invaluable asset to you with every online course you take.

Blackboard Student Manual http://www.blackboard.com/
eCollege Student Manual http://ecollege.com/
WebCT Student Orientation Center http://webct.com/

7 Online No No's

Online Students Ought to Know:

97. that **material that is specially placed on reserve for your course may not be shared outside the course**. Your course instructor may collect articles and even chapters from books for you to read as part of the course. The agreement to do this follows the laws and procedures of copyright law. You may also have access to special databases that are licensed to the institution offering your online course. In addition, your instruc-

tor may have placed book chapters and articles on reserve in an electronic library, which you access with a special username and password. All these materials are licensed for use by the instructor, you, and your fellow students for the duration of the online course. They must not be shared with anyone not registered in your online course.

Online Students Ought to Know:

98. that **you do not share your user name and password with anyone**. Just as you register to attend a traditional class, you register with your username and password to participate in an online course. It is important that you do not allow anyone else to access your course by giving them your username and password.

Online Students Ought to Know:

99. that **you do not alienate your student peers or instructor**. In online communication, you don't see another human being as you would in face to face interaction. You do not see any facial expressions or any gestures. You do not hear a voice with its special way of conveying emotions. All that you see is a computer monitor. Yet you must always consider the other person along with his or her feelings whenever you type an email, participate in keyboard chatting, or make comments

about an assignment. Do not make fun of or "flame" your instructor or fellow students when you communicate online. When in doubt, save your email and read it again later. That my take the "oops" out of email miscommunications and avoid hard feelings for the weeks remaining in the course.

Online Students Ought to Know:

100. that **you do not follow interesting but course irrelevant links when working on course assignments**. You must be task focused when doing your course assignments on the Internet. It is too easy to get sidetracked when you are on the Internet. You may be tempted to follow links that have little or nothing to do with the reason that you are researching the Internet. You may get so hypnotized with all that exciting information on the Internet that you forget what you are researching as you follow link after exciting link. Do not confuse play time or exploration time with course related task time.

Online Students Ought to Know:

101. that **you do not forget to abide by the basic rules of email etiquette**. Just as you follow conventions and rules when you write letters, you need to observe the rules and conventions of email. These have been called "netiquette." Netiquette includes respecting other student's privacy and viewpoints, being forgiving of other student's mistakes as you hope they will forgive yours, being aware of Internet hoaxes, viruses, and copyright violations.

Virginia Shea's Core Rules of Netiquette
http://www.albion.com/netiquette/book/index.html

Online Students Ought to Know:

102. that **you do not consider the Internet as the only research tool for your online course assignments**. The Internet is only a part of the whole information scene. Answers to course questions and problems can be found in print and audiovisual materials. Unless the institution offering your online course has licensed course material for your use, most books are not available on the Internet except as citations although sometimes a web site will place a book's table of contents and a sample chapter on a web page for your viewing.

Online Students Ought to Know:

One final item
Every online student ought to know that Cambridge Stratford, the publisher of this little book, has also published in its "100 Things" series two other books that can be helpful for you:
100 Things Every College Freshman Ought To Know
100 Things Every Adult Learner Ought To Know

Go to www.cambridgestratford.com or contact your local or online bookstore for further information.

8 Guidance from Online Students

Quote: *"There is only one simple thing that an online student must know. They must know organization. There is no other way of succeeding in an online class if you don't stay organized. Trust me, I know. A good portion of my classes have been online and I have remained a 4.0 student through it all. This was due to organization."* **-West Hills College Online Student**

The following admonitions and comments come from other online students at different colleges.

8.1   Keep up!

8.2   Be diligent and timely!

8.3   You must be a motivated self-learner.

8.4   Requires MORE time than traditional classes!

8.5   Online courses are NOT self-paced. Be ready to do weekly work and make weekly contributions.

8.6   Manage your time and be consistently organized.

8.7   Be dedicated and persistent.

8.8   Explore your courseware prior to beginning the course.

8.9   Know how to manage time, prioritize, and work independently.

8.10 Your instructor is there for you.

8.11 You need the ability to use your time wisely, push yourself, and avoid procrastination.

8.12 Watch out for the P word . . . Procrastination!

8.13 In order to succeed in an online course, you must be able to hold yourself accountable.

8.14 You must be disciplined throughout the whole course. If you start something, finish it.

8.15 READING guarantees success in all your online endeavors!!!!

8.16 The importance of staying focused and turning in assignments on time is very important.

8.17 Get a feel for the overall content and expectations of the course before you begin.

8.18 You need to ask yourself if you are comfortable in a less social situation and enjoy thinking independently.

8.19 Be ready to learn like you have never learned before!

8.20 You are a vital and essential member of your online course and you can help to build a sense of virtual community and help to enhance the overall learning environment.

8.21 Organization prior and during your online course is crucial to your success.

8.22 Online courses are convenient and flexible, but very demanding!

8.23 Online courses are great for working parents, military, and busy working adults—you can access your course from anywhere as long as you have a computer and a phone line.

8.24 You must be 'involved' in your online course!

8.25 WOW! I've never learned so much! More learning takes place with online courses versus traditional courses.

Conclusion

We mentioned in the introduction that one of the most critical skills for the online student is reading. We guarantee that after reading and mastering the skills and knowledge contained in this book, you will be a successful online student. This book offers the skills and knowledge that will empower you, the online student, and set you up for success in the online learning environment. In reading this book you have gained the awareness of skills and knowledge from hundreds of online students before you. These online students have discovered what is essential to their survival and success. Many of the practical items in *100 Things Every Online Student Ought to Know* come from online students who have learned from their real world experience. We welcome your reactions and comments. An Editorial Contribution form is attached at the end. Please share your comments so other online students in the future can learn from your online experiences. Remember the intent of the book is to empower you, the online student, to be successful as you pursue online courses. You are encouraged to keep *100 Things Every Online Student Ought to Know* by your computer for continuous reference. Please tell your fellow online students about the practical *100 Things Every Online Student Ought to Know*. Now get out there and have a successful and enjoyable learning experience as an online student!

Appendix

Editor Contribution Form
Glossary of Online Terms and Phases
Webliography
Works Consulted
Index
About the Publishiner

Editorial Comments and Contribution Pages

Dear Reader,

Your comments can help other adult college students make a smoother transition to college. Please share your thoughts, ideas, and suggestions on the following pages or on a separate sheet of paper. Also, fill in the biographical information below. I'll include a special reference by-line in my next edition to acknowledge all contributors. Thank you!

Name _____

Institution _____

City_____ State_____ Zip_____

☐ *Student*
☐ *Faculty*
☐ *Administrator*
☐ *Family/Friend*
☐ _____

(Cut or tear out form or e-mail to Cambridges@aol.com)

© 2003 by Cambridge Stratford, LTD.

My thoughts, ideas, and suggestions are

_____

_____

_____

_____

_____

_____

_____

_____

_____

_____

_____

(Cut or tear out form or e-mail to Cambridges@aol.com)

_____

_____

_____

_____

_____

_____

_____

_____

_____

Mail To: Dr. Loyd R. Ganey, Jr.
             c/o The Cambridge Stratford Study Skills Institute
             8560 Main Street
             Williamsville, NY 14221

(Cut or tear out form or e-mail to Cambridges@aol.com)

Glossary of Online Terms and Phrases

[Note: This glossary contains only terms and phrases used but not defined in this book. For other technical terms and phrases that may be used in discussions and articles about distance education, consult the following web sites:

Glossary of Internet Terms at http://www.luminet.net/~jackp/gloss2.htm

IOL: Glossary of Terms at
http://www.ion.illinois.edu/IONresources/onlinelearning/glossary.html

24/7. Twenty-four hours a day, seven days a week. Used to describe the hours of operation of online courses   or how often technical support is available for online students and teachers.

Bookmarks. Used to describe a way to quickly locate a site on the Internet with a web browser. After the bookmark is saved with its address (URL), users need not type in the address for access but just click on the bookmark.

Browser. Software, like Microsoft Internet Explorer or Netscape Navigator, used to navigate the web

CD-ROM. Used to describe an optical disk capable of storing large amounts of information.

Configuration. Used to describe how a computer or computer software is set up.

Courseware. The software used to view and interact with an online course. Some examples are Blackboard, eCollege, and WebCT

Cyber. Used as a synonym for web or Internet such as in cybercafe, cyberbuddy, or cyberspace,

Digital Drop Box. A location in Blackboard where students send their assignments for instructor viewing.

Discussion Board.   Also known as threaded discussion forums or message boards. These are places in online courseware where students and instructors post their thoughts on a given topic, statement or question and read what others have to say.

Diskette. A storage device to hold computer information. It may be a floppy, a zip disk, or a compact disk (CD).

Distance Education. Education that takes place with the Instructor and student in different locations.

Download. Used to describe the retrieval of a copy of a file from another computer. See also upload

Draft Folder. A special folder that contains emails that have been written but not yet sent.

Electronic Library. A collection of articles or other material that is stored on a library computer for access by online students and instructors.

External Link. A URL that takes you to another web page or web site.

Face to Face. Also written as F2F describes traditional classroom instruction

Flame. An Internet term used to describe language that may offend the recipient of an email.

Folder. Used to describe a computer object that can contain multiple documents or files.

Forum. See Discussion Board

Home Page. A page that a student designs that shows other students what he/she looks like and gives some personal information about him/her.

Internet Service Provider (ISP) A company like AOL or Earthlink that provides access to the Internet.

Live Chat. Online communication between two or more online persons either by keyboarding or voice.

MS Word. A word processing software developed by Microsoft.

Netiquette. The etiquette or rules of behavior for the Internet.

Offline. Not on the Internet.

Online.   On the Internet.

Password. A series of letters and numbers that a student creates for personal access a restricted web site.

PowerPoint. Software that creates a visual presentation or slide show.

Proctor. Someone who oversees students taking tests

Rich Text File (rtf). A word file that is formatted with special characteristics like lines, boxes, and special fonts.

Search Engine. A software program that searches the web for specific resources

Spam. Email that is sent to a recipient without authorization. Usually advertisements.

Streaming Audio. Used to describe a technique in which sound is transmitted rapidly from one computer to another.

Syllabus. A document that describes an academic course.

Threaded Discussion. See Discussion Board

Upload. Used to describe the transfer of a file from one computer to another. See download.

URL (Universal Resource Locator). The Internet address of a web page.

Username the name that you use to access your online course. Also written as userid

Virtual. Used to describe something on the Internet like a virtual guest, virtual faculty office, virtual library.

Web Page. A single screen of information.

Web Site. A collection of linked pages.

Whiteboard. An application that enables two or more users to share a Web-based 'chalkboard' device.

Zip Drive. A high-capacity disk drive that can hold more than fifty times more information than a regular diskette.

Webliography
A list of web sites referenced in each chapter

Introduction
Integrated Postsecondary Education Data System (IPEDS) College Opportunities
Online http://nces.ed.gov/ipeds/cool/Search.asp
Telecampus http://courses.telecampus.edu/subjects/index.cfm

Chapter 1   Online Facts
National Center for Educational Statistics http://www.nces.ed.gov/
Distance-Educator.Com http://www.distance-educator.com/
Council for Higher Education Accreditation http://www.chea.org/

Regional Accrediting Organizations
http://www.chea.org/Directories/regional.cfm
Virtual University Gazette's FAQs on Distance Learning, Accreditation, and College
Degrees http://www.geteducated.com/articles/dlfaq.htm
CollegeDegree.Com http://www.collegedegree.com/
Degree.Net http://www.degree.net/
Directory of Internet Universities http://www.geteducated.com/dlsites.htm
Distance Learning: Online Degrees
http://distancelearn.about.com/mbody.htm?once=true&
eLearners.Com http://www.elearners.com/
Yahoo! Directory>Distance Learning>Colleges and Universities
http://dir.yahoo.com/Education/Distance_Learning/Colleges_and_Universities/
Capella University http://www.capella.edu/schools_home_page/final.asp

Cochise College http://xwing.cochise.edu/online-campus/

Kaplan College http://www.kaplancollege.com

Western Governors University http://www.wgu.edu

Western International University http://www.wintu.edu

FinAid http://www.finaid.org/

Financial Aide Resource Center http://www.theoldschool.org/

The Student Guide: Financial Aide from the U.S. Department of Education 2002-2003
http://www.ed.gov/prog_info/SFA/StudentGuide/2002-3/index.html

Distance Education Glossary
http://www.utexas.edu/cc/cit/de/deprimer/glossary.html

Distance Learning Glossary http://www.wested.org/tie/dlrn/course/glossary.html

Blackboard http://blackboard.com/

eCollege http://ecollege.com/

WebCT http://webct.com

The Distance Education and Training Council http://www.detc.org/

Chapter 2   Online Access

eLearners.Com http://www.elearners.com/search/courses.asp

Online Course Directory http://www.aln.org/coursedirectory/

TeleCampus Online Course Directory http://www.telecampus.edu

Chapter 3   Online Preparation, Satisfaction, & Success

Cochise College Readiness Assessment

http://www.cochise.edu/assessment/register.cfm

DeAnza College Distance Learning Questionnaire

http://distance.deanza.fhda.edu/DLCQuestionnaire.shtml

Amazon. Com http://www.amazon.com

Barnes and Noble. Com http://barnesandnoble.com/
BigWords.Com http://www.bigwords.com/
BookFinder.Com http://www.bookfinder.com
eCampus.Com http://www.ecampus.com
Powell's Bookstore http://www.powells.com
Textbookx.Com http://www.textbookx.com
VarsityBooks.Com http://www.varsitybooks.com
AllTheWeb.Com http://www.alltheweb.com
Dogpile Multi-Search Engine http://www.dogpile.com
Google.Com http://www.google.com
Merlot.Org http://www.merlot.org
Northern Light http://www.northernlight.com
RDN Virtual Training Suite http://www.vts.rdn.ac.uk/

SearchEngineWatch.Com http://searchenginewatch.com/
Yahoo! Advanced Web Search http://search.yahoo.com/search/options

Chapter 4   Online Communications

Yale University Library - Email Etiquette
http://www.library.yale.edu/training/netiquette/
Email Etiquette - http://www.emailreplies.com/

Chapter 5 Online Learning and Study Skills & Strategies

Suggestions for Improving Reading Speed
http://www.ucc.vt.edu/stdysk/suggest.html
How to Improve Reading Comprehension
http://www.marin.cc.ca.us/~don/Study/7read.html

How Can I Organize My Textbook Reading? Or Unraveling The Textbook Maze
http://www.sla.purdue.edu/studentserv/learningcenter/handouts/txtvid94.htm
Critical reading strategies http://mind.phil.vt.edu/www/1204crs.html
How to Manage Time and Set Priorities:
http://www.marin.cc.ca.us/~don/Study/5time.html
Following directions
http://www.apurnell.com/images/FOLLOWING%20DIRECTIONS.htm
Professor Freedman's Math Help at http://www.mathpower.com/
Western Nebraska Community College Math Study Tips
http://hannibal.wncc.cc.ne.us/mathcenter/mathtips/index.html
Anthony Hughes' Online English Grammar
http://www.edufind.com/english/grammar/
Purdue University's Online Writing Lab http://owl.english.purdue.edu/

The Writing Center at the University of Wisconsin-Madison
http://www.wisc.edu/writing/
The New Century Handbook http://www.ablongman.com/hult
Study Guides and Strategies Webliography at
http://www.iss.stthomas.edu/studyguides/
Chemeketa CC Study Skills Resources http://www.howtostudy.org/resources.htm
Using Study Groups Effectively from the University of Dayton
http://academic.udayton.edu/aep/online/exams/study02.htm
Using study groups to increase learning
http://www.coun.uvic.ca/learn/program/hndouts/studygr.html
Online Teams http://www.learnntc.com/transition/teamwork.shtml
How to read essays you must analyze http://www.ucc.vt.edu/stdysk/essays.html

What is Plagiarism? A Short Concept Lesson by Ted Frick, Indiana University.
http://education.indiana.edu/~frick/plagiarism/
Evaluating Internet Research Sources http://www.virtualsalt.com/evalu8it.htm

Chapter 6   Online Student Support
Advice from "Those who Know" on Taking Weber State U-Online Courses
http://wsuonline.weber.edu/studsupport/sucess_stud/advice.htm
Asking questions - in class and out
http://www.chass.ncsu.edu/ccstm/scmh/questions.html
Do you never ask questions in class?
http://www.math.utah.edu/~alfeld/math/a22.html
Blackboard Student Manual http://www.blackboard.com/
Desire2Learn http:www.desire2learn.com
eCollege Student Services http://ecollege.com/student/STResources.html

WebCT Student Orientation Center http://webct.com/oriented

Chapter 7 Online No No's

The Core Rules of Netiquette

http://www.albion.com/netiquette/book/index.html http://www.albion.com/netiquette/corerules.html

Works Consulted

Basch, R. and Bates, M. E. (2000). **Researching Online for Dummies, 2nd Edition**. Foster City, CA: IDG Books Worldwide, Inc. ISBN 0-7645-0546-7. Comes with CD-ROM.

Connick, G. P. (Editor). (1999). **The Distance Learner's Guide**. Western Cooperative for Educational Telecommunications. Upper Saddle River, NJ: Prentice Hall.

Ganey, L. R. (2001). **Becoming a Successful Distance Learner: Eight Readiness Factors**. Clearwater, FL: H & H Publishing. ISBN 0-943202-76-0. (1-800-366-4079).

Gilbert, S. D. (2001). **How to Be a Successful Online Student**. New York, NY: McGraw-Hill.

Kramer, C. (2002). **Success in On-line Learning**. Albany, NY: Delmar/Thomson Learning.

McVay, M. (1998). **How to be a Successful Distance Student: Learning On the Internet**. Needham heights, MA: Pearson Custom Publishing.

Moran, A.P. (1997) **Managing Your Own Learning at University: A Practical Guide**. Dublin University College Press.

Pejsa, J. (1998). **Success in College Using the Internet**. Boston, MA: Houghton Mifflin Company.

Schlein, A. M. (2002). **Find It Online: The Complete Guide to Online Research, 3rd Edition**. Tempe, AZ: Facts On Demand Press. ISBN 1-889150-29-0.

Stevenson, N. (2000). **Distance Learning for Dummies**. Foster City, CA: IDG Books Worldwide, Inc.

Wahlstrom, C., Williams, B., and Shea, P. (2003). **The Successful Distance Learning Student**. Belmont, CA: Wadsworth/Thomson Learning.

Index by Item Number

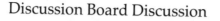

Discussion Board Discussion

Sally: Weblinks, indexes, glossaries, search engines; they certainly do strain my eyes and fingers. It's a lot of work and it makes me tired.

Sophie: As a 65 year old, so does walking. It would have taken me weeks to accomplish what I did this morning.

About the Publisher
The Cambridge Stratford Study Skills Institute

Cambridge Stratford, Ltd. formed The Cambridge Stratford Study Skills Institute in 1985 with the help of its current president, Peter W. Stevens, a former vice president from a private college in New York. It is an international organization of learning and study skills specialists and tutor training professionals dedicated to helping students of all ages to STUDY SMARTER, READ FASTER and SCORE HIGHER ON TESTS, key ingredients for success in school as well as in life.

Cambridge Stratford Study Skills Course System

The CSSS INSTITUTE provides teacher and tutor training services, private courses for students in summer and after school programs nationally, and publishes the internationally renowned study skills curriculum entitled **The Cambridge Stratford Study Skills Course**. It is taught publicly by schools, colleges, federal and state grant programs at 3 levels (6–8th: 20 hour edition, 9–11th: 30 hour edition, and 12–15th: 10 hour edition, entitled *Ten Tips for Academic Success*, available in English and Spanish). These editions include 4 components; Student Workbook, Teacher Manual, Transparency and Listening Tape Set.

Tutor Training Research Study

In 1994, The INSTITUTE introduced a research-based tutor training curriculum nationally under the direction of Dr. Ross MacDonald entitled *The Master Tutor: A Guidebook for More Effective Tutoring*. It includes the state-of-the-art methods tutors can use to improve one-on-one tutoring sessions and consists of a self-instructional Guidebook for tutors, a Tutor Trainer's Manual, and Transparency Set. A pre- and post-assessment, **The TESAT** (Tutor Evaluation and Self-Assessment Tool) is available for validating improved tutoring skills.

Starting 2002-2003, the *Online eMaster Tutor Training Course* was introduced to assist tutor trainers in training peer and staff tutors online. A train-the-trainer course, the *Online eMaster Tutor Trainer's Course*, was also made available to train online instructors in effectively teaching tutors using a hybrid of face-to-face and online instructional components.

Improving the Retention of College Students

The CSSS INSTITUTE's mission is to help students prepare for and succeed in college. In addition to this newest book for online students, two other self-orientation to college books have been published to help traditional and non-traditional adult college-bound students adjust to the difficult transitions required in becoming a successful college student. These navigation-to-college guidebooks, *100 Things Every Freshman Ought to Know* and *100 Things Every Adult College Student Ought to Know*, are suggested reading for all those starting college for the first time as well as those who may be returning to college after a lapse in time. Pre college and college preparation programs may find them helpful in building college persistence and retention among their students since each assists students in understanding college customs, practices, vocabulary, and procedures, plus each includes important tips for balancing responsibilities in college, family, and work environments. New editions of the *100 Things* series are being planned to include international students, disabled students, and those in the military.

NOTE: Prospective Authors — The *100 Things* series can be expanded to help others. If you have an idea, book, or concept that might help students succeed in school or college, please contact us at the address on the next page or via e-mail. We're interested!

If you need information about any of the products or services offered or would like a sample lesson (PREVIEW MANUAL) forwarded for your review, write or call today.

The Cambridge Stratford Study Skills Institute
8560 Main Street
Williamsville, New York 14221
(716) 626-9044 or FAX (716) 626-9076
Cambridges@aol.com
http://www.cambridgestratford.com